A-Z LOUGHB

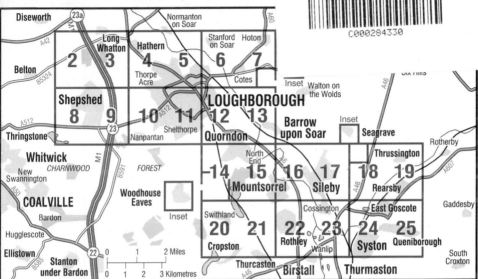

C000284330

Reference

Motorway	**M1**	Residential Walkway	Car Park — **P**
A Road	A60	Railway — Level Crossing / Station	Church or Chapel — †
Under Construction			Fire Station — ■
Proposed		Built Up Area — MILL ST	Hospital — **H**
B Road	B676	Local Authority Boundary	House Numbers — 83 96 (A & B Roads only)
Dual Carriageway		Posttown Boundary (By arrangement with the Post Office)	Information Centre — **i**
One Way A Roads (Traffic flow is indicated by a heavy line on the Driver's left.)	→	Postcode Boundary (Within Posttown)	National Grid Reference — ⁴54
Pedestrianized Road			Police Station — ▲
Restricted Access		Map Continuation — 14	Post Office — ★
Track			Toilet — ▽
Footpath		Ambulance Station — ✚	with facilities for the Disabled — ♿

Scale 1:15,840
4 inches to 1 mile

0 ¼ ½ ¾ Mile
0 250 500 750 Metres 1 Kilometre

Geographers' A-Z Map Co. Ltd.

Head Office : Fairfield Road, Borough Green, Sevenoaks, Kent TN15 8PP Telephone 01732 781000
Showrooms : 44 Gray's Inn Road, Holborn, London WC1X 8HX Telephone 0171-242-9246

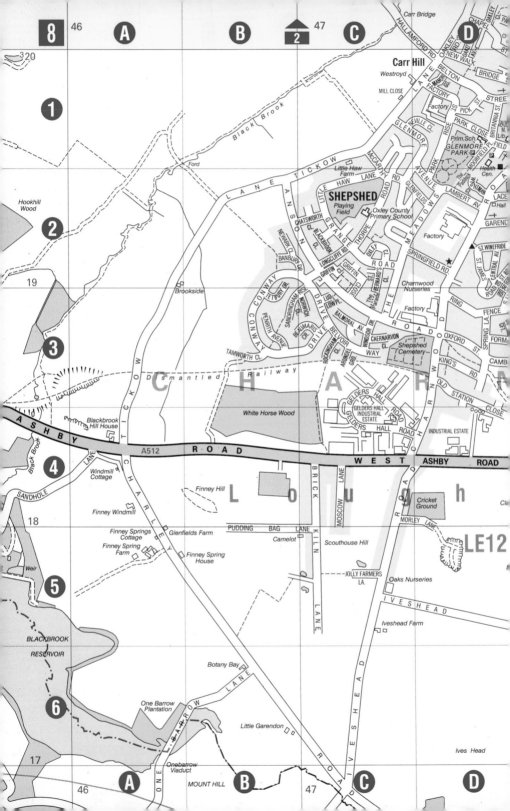

E **F** 57 **G** **H** 58 **13**

Brook Farm
7
Brook Fields Farm
NOTTINGHAM RD

Walton Grange
Walton Lodge
Walton Brook
3 20

1

Walton Holme
Hunter's Lodge
WALTON ROAD

Walton Holme Farm
Fieldfares
BARROW HILL

Coteswick Farm

Barrow Barn

2

Ryecroft Farm

o r o u g h

Foxhill Farm
19

3

Navigation
Top Bridge

LE12
Drain
CATSICK HILL
Glenworth Farm
STRANCLIFFE LANE

4

Pilling's Lock
Weir
Towing Path
Chapel
COTES ROAD
STRANCLIFFE LANE
BARROW-UPON-SOAR
Cricket Club
Pev.
FISHPOOL

Cemetery
Pig Farm
Strancliffe
18

Works
W O O D
RIVER SOAR
Tennis Court
Playing Field
Comm. Cen.
Humphrey Perkins High School
King George's Field
BROOKSIDE

5

Drain
Meadow Farm
Playing Field
BEAUMONT
Lib
Church St.
BRYAN CL.
BREADCROFT
THE RETREAT

Poole Farm
HOVEL LANE
The Bungalow
WOODSIDE ROAD
CHURCH ST.
Hall Orchard C. of E. Prim. Sch.
HIGHFIELDS

Pumping Station
SORREL ROAD
BARROW ROAD
Lodge
Health Cen.
HIGH ST.
BEVERIDGE ST.
NEW ST.
MELTON ROAD

Sports Ground
CAUSEWAY
BRIDGE ST.
CRANLEY
SOUTH ST.
WARNER ST.
GROVE LA.
BRACKYFIELD
CON. DOM. RD.

6

BY-PASS
Barrow Lock
PROCTORS
SOUTH MILL LANE
SILEBY ROAD

Barrow-upon-Soar

Drain
PROCTOR'S PLEASURE PARK
Towing Path
Quorn Hall
MARTIN LANE
PUDDLE DR.
CHERWELL RD.

QUORNDON (Quorn)

E **F** **15** 57 **G** **H** 58
WELLAND RD.

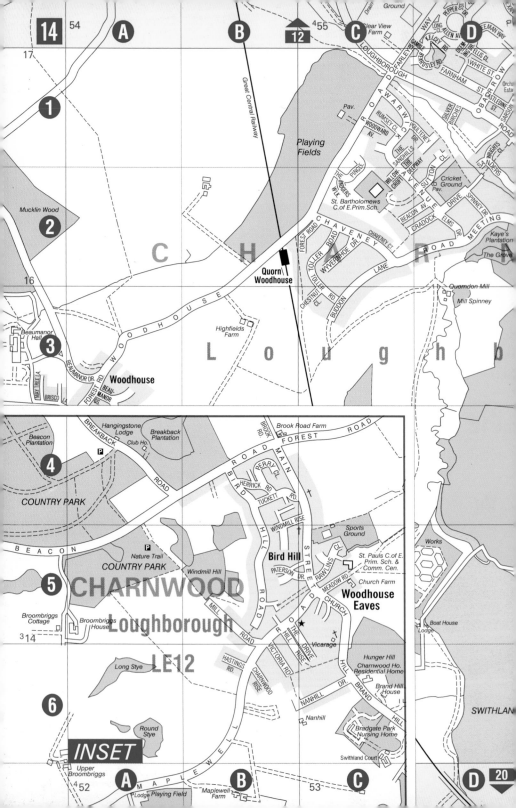

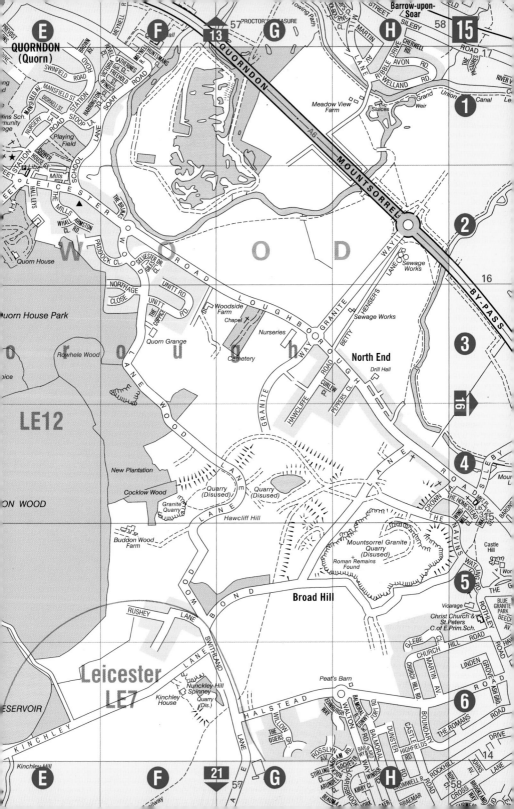

1

PARK HILL
GOLF
COURSE

2

Canbyfield
Lodge

Belle Isle

Hanover Lodge

o   r   o   u   g   h

16

JUBILEE AV.
RISE
ROAD
Highgate
Prim. Sch.

Pryor
HEATHCOTE
GREEDON RISE
FOREST DR.
BARRADALE AV.
HUDSON RD.
GREEDON
COLLINGWOOD DRIVE
DICKENS CL.
MELDON AV.
BRUSHFIELD AV.
NEWBOLD ROAD
LANES CL.
PARSONS DR.
Highgate Farm

3

HOMEFIELD
PARK ROAD
ST. MARY'S RD.
ALBERT AV.
GREEDON RISE
SPRINGFIELD RD.
MARSHALL AV.
PODDIN WAY
MOREM CL.
NICKLE CL.
DALE
GIBSON ST.
HANOVER DR.
SMITH CL.
CLEATHCOTE DR.
BARNARDS DR.
STANAGE RD.
NORTH HILL CL.
AINSWORTH DR.
DRIVE

Factory
Playing Field
Redlands Prim. Sch.
Factory
SILEBY MEMORIAL PARK
War Memorial
Pav.
SILEBY
ST. GREGORY'S DR.
DAUBY CL.
FINSBURY AV.
ROAD

18

SILEBY RD.
INDUSTRIAL
ESTATE
STREET SWAN
HIGHGATE STREET
Works
WELLBROOK DR.
CLAIRE CL.
PEASHILL CL.
CLIFFE

4

HIGH KING
CHURCH ST.
BROOK
BACK LA.
DUDLEY CL.
ALBION RD.
THE RANKS
BANKS
WARDS
CEMETERY ROAD
Factory
STONER
Cemetery
Chapel
PEASHILL CL.

Peas Hill Farm

Th 3115 Farm

e Hall
Library
MANOR
DRIVE
ALBION ROAD
KENDAL
KENDAL CL.
STAVELEY CL.
PHOENIX DR.
Depot

Peas Hill Farm
The Lodge

Factory
KILBOURNE RD.
MILNER
FLAXLAND CR.
CHARLES
SHERRARD DR.
WALLACE ST.
CHARLES ST.
CHARLES ST.
MULLINEUX DR.
Blossom Farm

5

CROSSINGTON
QUAKER
CHALFONT
W. ORCHD.
EAST CL.
OAK GDNS.
DRIVE
ROAD

Leicester

LE7

Poultry Houses
Reservoir (Cove

ROAD

6

Brook Farm
Nursery
MAIN ST.

BLACKBERRY LANE

Glebe Lodge Farm

HUMBLE LANE

Humbles Farm
Shepherds Crook

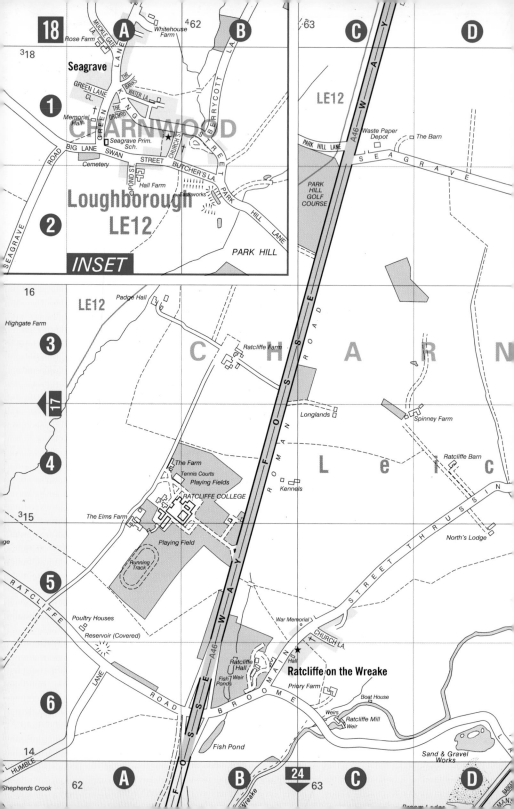

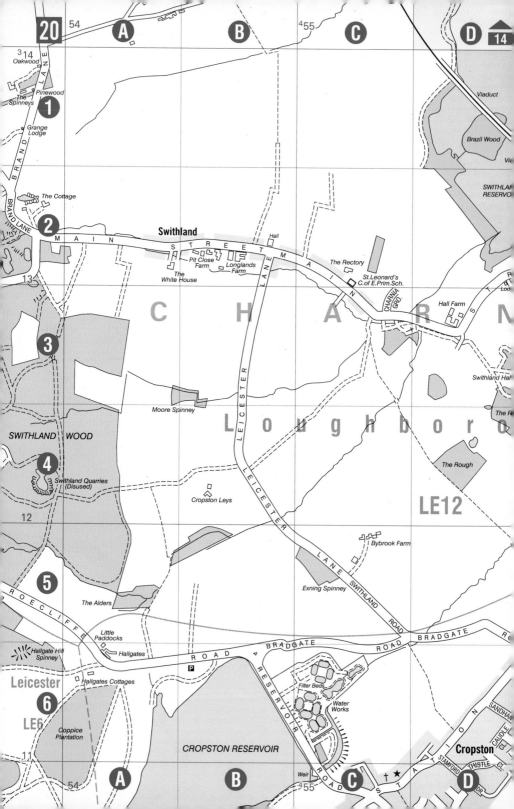

³14
Oakwood

1

The Spinneys   Pinewood

Grange Lodge

BRAND LANE

2

The Cottage

13

M A I N   S T R E E T

Swithland

Pit Close Farm
The White House
Longlands Farm
Hall

LANE

The Rectory

St.Leonard's C.of E.Prim.Sch.

CHARNIA GRD.

Hall Farm

C H A R N

3

Moore Spinney

MAIN

SWITHLAND WOOD

Leicester

L o u g h b o r o

LE12

Swithland Hall

The R

The Rough

4

Swithland Quarries (Disused)

Cropston Leys

LEICESTER LANE

Bybrook Farm

12

5

The Alders

ROECLIFFE

Exning Spinney

SWITHLAND ROAD

Little Paddocks

Hallgate Hill Spinney

Hallgates

ROAD

BRADGATE   ROAD   BRADGATE   RO

Leicester

6

Hallgates Cottages

P

RESERVOIR

Filter Beds

Water Works

SANDHA

LE6

Coppice Plantation

Cropston

11

CROPSTON RESERVOIR

Weir

STAMFORD

THISTLE

CAUDLE

DR.

54

Viaduct

Brazil Wood

Vi

SWITHLAN RESERVO

Lo

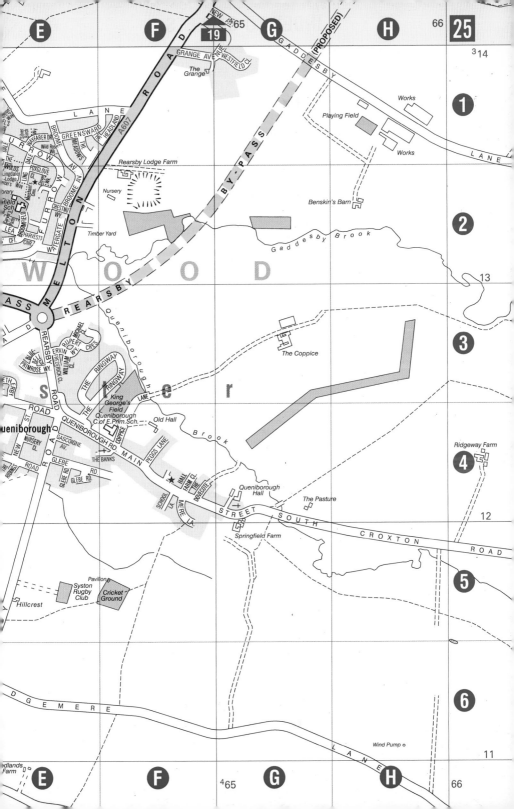

INDEX TO STREETS

HOW TO USE THIS INDEX

1. Each street name is followed by its Posttown or Postal Locality and then by its map reference; e.g. Abberton Way. Lou —3A **10** is in the Loughborough Posttown and is to be found in square 3A on page **10**. The page number being shown in bold type. A strict alphabetical order is followed in which Av., Rd., St., etc. (though abbreviated) are read in full and as part of the street name; e.g. Ash Clo. appears after Ashby Sq. but before Ashdown Clo.

2. Streets and a selection of Subsidiary names not shown on the Maps, appear in the index in *Italics* with the thoroughfare to which it is connected shown in brackets; e.g. *George Deacon Ct. Lou —2G* **11** *(off Ashby Rd.)*

GENERAL ABBREVIATIONS

All : Alley
App : Approach
Arc : Arcade
Av : Avenue
Bk : Back
Boulevd : Boulevard
Bri : Bridge
B'way : Broadway
Bldgs : Buildings
Bus : Business
Cen : Centre
Chu : Church
Chyd : Churchyard
Circ : Circle
Cir : Circus

Clo : Close
Comn : Common
Cotts : Cottages
Ct : Court
Cres : Crescent
Dri : Drive
E : East
Embkmt : Embankment
Est : Estate
Gdns : Gardens
Ga : Gate
Gt : Great
Grn : Green
Gro : Grove
Ho : House

Ind : Industrial
Junct : Junction
La : Lane
Lit : Little
Lwr : Lower
Mnr : Manor
Mans : Mansions
Mkt : Market
M : Mews
Mt : Mount
N : North
Pal : Palace
Pde : Parade
Pk : Park
Pas : Passage

Pl : Place
Rd : Road
S : South
Sq : Square
Sta : Station
St : Street
Ter : Terrace
Up : Upper
Vs : Villas
Wlk : Walk
W : West
Yd : Yard

POSTTOWN AND POSTAL LOCALITIES ABBREVIATIONS

Bar S : Barrow upon Soar
Bur W : Burton on the Wolds
Char : Charley
Costn : Cossington
Cotes : Cotes
Crop : Cropston
E Gos : East Goscote
Hath : Hathern

Hot : Hoton
Long W : Long Whatton
Lou : Loughborough
Mount : Mountsorrel
Nan : Nanpantan
Nor S : Normanton on Soar
Pres : Prestwold
Quen : Queniborough

Quor : Quorndon
Rat W : Ratcliffe on the Wreake
Rear : Rearsby
Roth : Rothley
Sea : Seagrave
Shep : Shepshed
Sile : Sileby
Stan S : Stanford on Soar

Swit : Swithland
Sys : Syston
Thrus : Thrussington
Thurc : Thurcaston
Wan : Wanlip
Wood : Woodhouse
Wood E : Woodhouse Eaves

INDEX TO STREETS

Abberton Way. Lou —3A **10**
Abbotts Clo. Sys —6H **23**
Acer Clo. Lou —6G **11**
Adkins Way. Bar S —5H **13**
Afton Clo. Lou —2B **10**
Ainsworth Dri. Sile —3G **17**
Alan Moss Rd. Lou —1D **10**
Albany St. Lou —6E **5**
Albert Av. Sile —3F **17**
Albert Pl. Lou —2H **11**
Albert Promenade. Lou —2A **12**
Albert St. Lou —2H **11**
Albert St. Sys —6B **24**
Albion Pde. Sys —6B **24**
Albion Rd. Sile —4E **17**
Albion St. Sys —6B **24**
Alexander Rd. Quor —6D **12**
Alfred St. Lou —6H **5**
Allen Av. Quor —6D **12**
Allsop's La. Lou —6B **6**
Alston Dri. Lou —5D **4**
Althorpe Dri. Lou —6C **4**
Ambleside Clo. Lou —5D **10**
Amis Clo. Lou —6C **4**
Anchor Clo. Hath —3A **4**
Anchor La. Hath —2A **4**
Angel Yd. Lou —1H **11**
Angus Dri. Lou —1D **10**
Anson Rd. Shep —2B **8**
Anstey La. Thurc —6F **21**
Anthony St. Roth —3A **22**
Arbury Dale. Shep —3E **9**
Archdale St. Sys —6H **23**

Archer Clo. Lou —5B **4**
Archers Grn. E Gos —2D **24**
Armitage Clo. Lou —1G **11**
Armston Rd. Quor —2E **15**
Arthur St. Lou —2G **11**
Arundel Clo. Mount —1G **21**
Arundel Gro. Shep —3C **8**
Ashby Cres. Lou —2D **10**
Ashby Rd. Lou —1E **11**
Ashby Rd. Shep & Long W
—4A **2**
Ashby Rd. Central. Shep —4D **8**
Ashby Rd. E. Shep —4E **9**
Ashby Rd. W. Shep —4A **8**
Ashby Sq. Lou —1G **11**
Ash Clo. Bar S —4H **13**
Ashdown Clo. Lou —6C **4**
Ash Gro. Hath —2A **4**
Ash Gro. Mount —6A **16**
Ashleigh Dri. Lou —3E **11**
Aspen Av. Lou —6G **11**
Atherstone Rd. Lou —6F **11**
Aumberry Gap. Lou —1H **11**
Avenue Clo. Quen —4E **25**
Avenue Rd. Quen —4E **25**
Avenue Rd. Sile —5E **17**
Avery Dri. Sys —4B **24**
Avon Rd. Bar S —1H **15**
Avon Vale Rd. Lou —4A **12**

Babington Ct. Roth —3A **22**
Babington Rd. Bar S —5H **13**

Babington Rd. Roth —3A **22**
Back La. Costn —2F **23**
Back La. Cotes —5D **6**
Back La. Sile —4E **17**
Back La. Thrus —3F **19**
Badger Ct. Lou —5D **10**
Badgers Bank. Roth —2A **22**
Badger's Corner. E Gos
—1D **24**
Badgers Wlk. Quor —2C **14**
Badminton Rd. Sys —4B **24**
Bagley Clo. Lou —5C **4**
Bailey Clo. Lou —5D **10**
Bainbridge Rd. Lou —4A **12**
Bakewell Rd. Lou —4E **5**
Balliol Av. Sys —6C **24**
Balmoral Av. Shep —3C **8**
Balmoral Rd. Mount —6H **15**
Bampton St. Lou —2H **11**
Banbury Dri. Shep —2B **8**
Banks Clo., The. Sile —4E **17**
Banks, The. Bar S —5H **13**
Banks, The. Quen —4E **25**
Banks, The. Sea —1A **18**
Banks, The. Sile —4E **17**
Barden Clo. Lou —5D **10**
Barkby Rd. Quen —6E **25**
Barkby Rd. Sys —5B **24**
Barley Way. Roth —2A **22**
Barnards Dri. Sile —3G **17**
Barnard Way. Mount —6H **15**
Barons Way. Mount —4A **16**
Barrack Row. Lou —6H **5**

Barradale Av. Sile —3E **17**
Barrett Dri. Lou —5D **4**
Barrowcliffe Clo. Bar S —5G **13**
Barrow Rd. Bur W —6G **7**
Barrow Rd. Cotes —5C **6**
Barrow Rd. Quor —1D **14**
Barrow Rd. Sile —2C **16**
Barrow St. Lou —2H **11**
Barry Dri. Sys —5B **24**
Barsby Dri. Lou —5D **4**
Bath St. Sys —5A **24**
Baxter Ga. Lou —1H **11**
Bayliss Clo. Quor —6D **12**
Beacon Av. Lou —4F **11**
Beacon Av. Quor —2C **14**
Beacon Dri. Lou —4G **11**
Beacon Rd. Lou —5F **11**
Beacon Rd. Wood E —5A **14**
Beardsley Rd. Quor —1D **14**
Beatty Rd. Sys —5B **24**
Beaufort Av. Lou —5G **11**
Beaumanor Dri. Wood —3A **14**
Beaumanor Gdns. Wood
—3A **14**
Beaumaris Cres. Shep —3C **8**
Beaumaris Rd. Mount —1G **21**
Beaumont Rd. Bar S —5G **13**
Beaumont Rd. Lou —5H **11**
Bedford Sq. Lou —2H **11**
Bedford St. Lou —2H **11**
Beeby Clo. Sys —6C **24**
Beeches Av. Mount —5A **16**
Beeches Rd. Lou —3A **12**

Beechwood Av. Quen —4D **24**
Bee Hive La. Lou —2H **11**
Belmont Way. Lou —3A **10**
Belton Rd. Lou —6G **5**
Belton Rd. W. Lou —5E **5**
Belton Rd. W. Extension. Lou
—5F **5**
Belton St. Shep —1D **8**
Belvoir Clo. Mount —1H **21**
Belvoir Dri. Lou —6F **11**
Belvoir Dri. Sys —5C **24**
Belvoir Way. Shep —3C **8**
Bennetts La. Costn —1F **23**
Benscliffe Dri. Lou —3E **11**
Beresford Ct. Shep —1E **9**
Berkeley Clo. Mount —6B **16**
Berkeley Clo. Pk. Homes. Mount
—6A **16**
Berkeley Rd. Lou —5C **10**
Berrycott La. Sea —1B **18**
Betty Henser's La. Mount
—3H **15**
Beveridge St. Bar S —6H **13**
Biggin St. Lou —1H **11**
Big La. Sea —1A **18**
Birch Av. Bar S —4H **13**
Bird Hill Rd. Wood E —4B **14**
Bishop Meadow Rd. Lou —5E **5**
Bishop St. Lou —1A **12**
Blackberry La. Costn —1G **23**
Blackbrook Clo. Shep —2C **8**
Blackbrook Ct. Lou —5E **5**
Blackbrook Rd. Lou —2C **10**
Blackham Rd. Lou —4G **11**
Blacksmiths Av. Shep —6E **3**
Blackthorn Dri. Sys —5H **23**
Blair Clo. Mount —1H **21**
Blake Dri. Lou —6D **4**
Bleakmoor Clo. Rear —4G **19**
Blenheim Clo. Lou —1C **10**
Blithfield Av. Lou —2C **10**
Bluebell Clo. Quen —3E **25**
Bluebell Clo. Lou —4F **11**
Blue Granite Pk. Mount —5A **16**
Bond Clo. Lou —4A **12**
Bond La. Mount —5G **15**
Borrowdale Way. Lou —4D **10**
Bottleacre La. Lou —5G **5**
Boundary Rd. Mount —6H **15**
Boundary Way. Shep —6E **3**
Bowler Ct. Lou —2A **12**
Bowling Grn. Clo. Sile —3F **17**
Boyer St. Lou —1A **12**
Bracken Dale. E Gos —2E **25**
Braddon Rd. Lou —5C **4**
Bradgate Rd. Crop —6B **20**
Bradgate Rd. Lou —5E **11**
Braemar Clo. Mount —1H **21**
Bramcote Rd. Lou —6F **11**
Brand Hill. Wood E —6C **14**
Brand La. Wood —2A **20**
Branston Av. Bar S —5H **13**
Breachfield Rd. Bar S —6H **13**
Breadcroft La. Bar S —5H **13**
Breakback Rd. Wood E —4A **14**
Breech Hedge. Roth —2H **21**
Brendon Clo. Shep —4E **9**
Brick Kiln La. Shep —4C **8**
Brickwood Pl. Bur W —5G **7**
Bridge St. Bar S —6G **13**
Bridge St. Lou —1G **11**
Bridge St. Shep —1D **8**
Brighton Av. Sys —5C **24**

Brinks, The. Quor —2F **15**
Brisco Av. Lou —5F **5**
Brisco La. Lou —3A **14**
Britannia St. Shep —1D **8**
Broad St. Lou —1G **11**
Broad St. Sys —6A **24**
Broadway. Lou —5G **11**
Broadway. Sys —6A **24**
Bromhead St. Lou —6A **6**
Brookfield Av. Lou —4E **11**
Brookfield Av. Sys —6B **24**
Brookfield St. Sys —6B **24**
Brook Ho. Clo. Rear —6F **19**
Brookland Way. Mount —1A **22**
Brook La. Bar S —5H **13**
Brook La. Lou —5D **10**
Brook Rd. Wood E —4B **14**
Brookside. Rear —5G **19**
Brookside. Sys —5A **24**
(in two parts)
Brookside Clo. Bar S —5H **13**
Brookside Clo. Shep —3E **9**
Brookside Rd. Lou —5D **10**
Brook St. Bur W —5G **7**
Brook St. Rear —6G **19**
Brook St. Shep —1E **9**
Brook St. Sile —4E **17**
Brook St. Sys —5A **24**
Broom Av. Lou —6G **11**
Broome Av. E Gos —2E **25**
Broome La. Rat W —6B **18**
Broomfield. E Gos —2E **25**
Brown Av. Quor —6E **13**
Brownhill Cres. Roth —4F **21**
Browning Rd. Lou —1D **10**
Browns La. Lou —2G **11**
Brushfield Av. Sile —3F **17**
Bruxby St. Sys —6H **23**
Bryan Clo. Bar S —5H **13**
Buckhorn Sq. Lou —1A **12**
Buckingham Dri. Lou —6C **4**
Buddon La. Quor —3C **14**
Bull Ring. Shep —2D **8**
Bulrush Clo. Mount —6B **16**
Burbage Clo. Lou —5E **5**
Burder St. Lou —6A **6**
Burfield Av. Lou —2G **11**
Burleigh Fields. Lou —1F **11**
Burleigh Rd. Lou —1G **11**
Burns Rd. Lou —6D **4**
Burton St. Lou —3H **11**
Burton Walks. Lou —3H **11**
Burton Wlks. Lou —3H **11**
Butcher's La. Sea —2B **18**
Butterley Dri. Lou —3B **10**
Buttermere Way. Bar S —4G **13**
Butthole La. Shep —1E **9**
Butt La. Nor S —1D **4**
Byland Way. Lou —5B **4**
Byron St. Lou —6E **5**
Byron St. Extension. Lou —6E **5**

Cabin Leas. Lou —5H **5**
Caernarvon Clo. Mount —1H **21**
Caernarvon Clo. Shep —3C **8**
Caldwell St. Lou —1G **11**
Cambridge St. Lou —6H **5**
Cambridge St. Shep —3D **8**
Canal Bank. Lou —6G **5**
Canning Way. Lou —5C **4**
Carillon Clo. Lou —1H **11**
Carington St. Lou —6F **5**

Carisbrooke Rd. Mount —1H **21**
Cartland Dri. Lou —5C **4**
Cartwright St. Lou —6H **5**
Carver's Path. E Gos —2E **25**
Castledine Av. Quor —6D **12**
Castledine St. Lou —3H **11**
Castledine St. Quor —1D **14**
Castledine St. Extension. Lou
—3H **11**
Castle Hill. Mount —5A **16**
Castle Rd. Mount —6H **15**
Catherines Clo. Quor —1F **15**
Cattlemarket. Lou —1H **11**
Cauby Clo. Sile —4G **17**
Caudle Clo. Crop —6D **20**
Cave Rd. Bar S —5H **13**
Caxton Pl. Bar S —6H **13**
Cayley Hall. Lou —2D **10**
Cedar Rd. Lou —4A **12**
Cemetery Rd. Sile —4F **17**
Central Av. Shep —2D **8**
Central Av. Sys —5B **24**
Chainbridge Clo. Lou —6G **5**
Chalfont Dri. Sile —6E **17**
Challottee. Shep —2E **9**
Chapel Clo. Sys —5A **24**
Chapel Clo. Thurc —6F **21**
Chapel St. Shep —6D **2**
Chapel St. Shep —6D **2**
Chapel St. Sys —5A **24**
Chapman St. Lou —1A **12**
Charles St. Lou —6H **5**
Charles St. Sile —5E **17**
Charley Dri. Lou —3E **11**
Charley Rd. Shep —4A **8**
Charnia Gro. Swit —3C **20**
Charnwood Rise. Wood E
—6B **14**
Charnwood Rd. Lou —3H **11**
Charnwood Rd. Shep —4D **8**
Charteris Clo. Lou —5D **4**
Chase, The. E Gos —1D **24**
Chatsworth Clo. Lou —2C **8**
Chatsworth Dri. Sys —6H **23**
Chatsworth Rd. Lou —6D **4**
Chaveney Ct. Quor —2C **14**
Chaveney Rd. Quor —2C **14**
Chelker Way. Lou —2C **10**
Cherry Clo. Lou —6G **11**
Cherwell Rd. Bar S —6H **13**
Chester Clo. Lou —2F **11**
Chestnut Clo. Quen —4D **24**
Chestnut Clo. Quor —3C **14**
Chestnut Clo. Shep —2E **9**
Chestnut Clo. Sys —6B **24**
Chestnut St. Lou —1G **11**
Chestnut Way. E Gos —2E **25**
Cheviot Dri. Shep —2E **9**
Chichester Clo. Lou —5C **10**
Chiltern Av. Shep —2F **9**
Chiswick Dri. Lou —1C **10**
Christie Dri. Lou —5D **4**
Church Ga. Lou —1H **11**
Church Ga. Shep —1E **9**
Church Hill. Wood E —5C **14**
Church Hill Rd. Mount —6H **15**
Church Lands. Lou —5H **5**
Church La. Bar S —5H **13**
Church La. Quor —1E **15**
Church La. Rat W —5C **18**
Church La. Rear —5G **19**
Church La. Thrus —3F **19**
Church Leys Av. Rear —5G **19**

Church Rd. Wan —6E **23**
Church Side. Shep —1E **9**
Church St. Bar S —5H **13**
Church St. Hath —2A **4**
Church St. Roth —3B **22**
Church St. Sea —1A **18**
Church St. Shep —1D **8**
Claire Ct. Sile —4G **17**
Clarence St. Lou —6H **5**
Clawson Clo. Lou —5D **4**
Cleeve Mt. Lou —1C **10**
Cleveland Rd. Lou —6F **11**
Cliff Av. Lou —5F **5**
Clifford Rd. Lou —6F **5**
Cloud Lea. Mount —1A **22**
Clover La. Mount —6B **16**
Clover Wlk. E Gos —2E **25**
Clowbridge Dri. Lou —2C **10**
Clumber Clo. Sys —4B **24**
Coachmans Ct. Shep —6E **3**
Coach Rd. Shep —2F **9**
Cobden St. Lou —1A **12**
Coe Av. Lou —6B **4**
Colgrove Rd. Lou —3G **11**
College Rd. Sys —6B **24**
Collingwood Dri. Sile —3F **17**
Compton Clo. Lou —5C **10**
Condon Rd. Bar S —6H **13**
Coneries, The. Lou —1H **11**
Coniston Cres. Lou —4D **10**
Coniston Rd. Bar S —5H **13**
Connaught Clo. Roth —3A **22**
Conway Clo. Lou —6C **4**
Conway Dri. Shep —3B **8**
Conway Rd. Mount —6H **15**
Cookson Pl. Lou —5C **4**
Coombe Clo. Shep —3E **9**
Cooper Ct. Lou —3B **12**
Cooper's Nook. E Gos —2D **24**
Coplow Cres. Sys —6A **24**
Coppice La. Quen —4F **25**
Coppice, The. Quor —3F **15**
Cordell Rd. Lou —5F **5**
Cossington La. Costn —2H **23**
Cossington La. Roth —3C **22**
Cossington Rd. Sile —5E **17**
Cotes Rd. Cotes —5D **6**
Cothelstone Av. Lou —6C **4**
Cotswold Clo. Lou —2D **10**
Cottesmore Dri. Lou —6F **11**
Cotton Croft. Shep —3D **8**
Cotton Way. Lou —4E **5**
Countryman's Way. E Gos
—1D **24**
Countrymans Way. Shep —6E **3**
Covert Clo. Sys —5G **23**
Covert, The. E Gos —1D **24**
Cowdray Clo. Lou —4G **11**
Craddock Dri. Quor —2C **14**
Craddock St. Lou —1H **11**
Cramps Clo. Bar S —6H **13**
Cranmer Dri. Sys —6H **23**
Craven Clo. Lou —6F **11**
Cricket La. Lou —5D **10**
Cromwell Rd. Mount —1H **21**
Croome Clo. Lou —4A **12**
Cropston Av. Lou —3B **10**
Cross Grn. Roth —3A **22**
Cross Hedge. Roth —2A **22**
Cross Hill La. Lou —5F **11**
Cross La. Mount —1H **21**
Crossley Clo. Bar S —6G **13**
Cross St. Hath —2A **4**

Cross St. Lou —6A **6**
Cross St. Sys —6B **24**
Crosswood Clo. Lou —2C **10**
Crown La. Mount —4H **15**
Cumberland Rd. Lou —1F **11**
Cumberland Rd. Trading Est.
 Lou —1F **11**
Cumbrian Way. Shep —2E **9**
Curlew Clo. Mount —3G **15**
Curlew Clo. Sys —5G **23**
Curzon Clo. Quen —4D **24**
Curzon St. Lou —1G **11**
Cygnet Dri. Sys —5H **23**
Cypress Clo. Lou —6G **11**

Dalley Clo. Sys —6B **24**
Danvers La. Shep —1E **9**
Danvers Rd. Mount —6A **16**
Deacon Clo. Shep —2E **9**
Dead La. Lou —1H **11**
Deane St. Lou —6E **5**
Deanside Dri. Lou —5D **4**
Deeming Dri. Quor —6D **12**
Deepway, The. Quor —2C **14**
Deer Acre. Lou —5H **5**
Deighton Way. Lou —5C **4**
Delisle Ct. Lou —3B **10**
Demontfort Clo. Lou —6C **4**
Derby Rd. Hath —1H **3**
Derby Rd. Lou —4C **4**
Derby Sq. Lou —1H **11**
Derwent Dri. Lou —4D **10**
 (in two parts)
Derwent Rd. Bar S —5H **13**
Devonshire Sq. Lou —2H **11**
Dexter Clo. Quor —6D **12**
Dickens Clo. Sile —3F **17**
Disraeli St. Quor —1E **15**
Dobney Av. Quen —3C **24**
Dormer Ct. Hath —2A **4**
Dovecote. Shep —1E **9**
Dovecote St. Hath —2A **4**
Dovecote, The. Quen —4F **25**
Dower Ho. Gdns. Quor —1E **15**
Doyle Clo. Lou —5D **4**
Drive, The. Wood E —5B **14**
Dry Pot La. Long W —1A **2**
Dudley Ct. Sile —4E **17**
Duke St. Lou —6H **5**
Dulverton Clo. Lou —5C **10**
Duncan Way. Lou —5C **4**
Dunholme Av. Lou —1B **10**
Dunsmore Clo. Lou —5D **10**
Dunster Rd. Mount —6H **15**
Durham Rd. Lou —5E **5**
Durrell Clo. Lou —5C **4**

Easby Clo. Lou —6A **4**
East Av. Sys —6C **24**
E. Goscote Ind. Est. E Gos
 —2D **24**
E. Orchard. Sile —6E **17**
Edelin Rd. Lou —4H **11**
Eden Clo. Lou —6C **4**
Edinburgh Way. Mount —6G **15**
Edward St. Lou —6G **5**
Eggington Ct. Lou —3E **11**
Eliot Clo. Lou —5B **4**
Ellaby Rd. Lou —5D **4**
Ellis Clo. Bar S —5H **13**
Ellis Clo. Quor —1D **14**

Elm Clo. Mount —5A **16**
Elm Gdns. Mount —6A **16**
Elms Dri. Quor —2D **14**
Elms Gro. Bar S —4H **13**
Elms Gro. Lou —2A **12**
Elvyn Richards Hall. Lou
 —3D **10**
Empress Rd. Lou —1A **12**
Ennerdale Rd. Bar S —5H **13**
Epinal Way. Lou —6D **4**
Ervin Way. Quen —3E **25**
Essex Lodge. Lou —1F **11**
Eve Brook Clo. Lou —3B **10**
Exmoor Clo. Lou —5D **10**

Factory St. Lou —2A **12**
Factory St. Shep —1D **8**
Fairmead. Mount —1A **22**
Fairmeadows Way. Lou —6F **11**
Fairmount Dri. Lou —3E **11**
Fairway Rd. Shep —2E **9**
Fairway Rd. S. Shep —4E **9**
Falcon Clo. Lou —6A **6**
Falkner Ct. Lou —3E **11**
Faraday Hall. Lou —3D **10**
Farley Way. Quor —1C **14**
Farndale Dri. Lou —5F **11**
Farnham Clo. Roth —2A **22**
Farnham Rd. Lou —4H **11**
Farnham St. Quor —1D **14**
Farrier's Way. E Gos —2D **24**
Farthings, The. Hath —2A **4**
Fearon St. Lou —1F **11**
Fennel St. Lou —1H **11**
Ferneley Rise. Thrus —3F **19**
Festival Dri. Lou —5G **5**
Field Av. Shep —5E **3**
Field Crest. Mount —1H **21**
Field Ho. Lou —1E **11**
Field St. Shep —1D **8**
Field View. Sys —6G **23**
Finsbury Av. Lou —2A **12**
Finsbury Av. Sile —4G **17**
Fisher Clo. Costn —1F **23**
Fishpool Way. Bar S —4H **13**
Flattenway. Sys —5A **24**
Flaxland. Roth —2A **22**
Flaxland Cres. Sile —5E **17**
Fleming Clo. Lou —5D **4**
Flesh Hovel La. Quor —4E **13**
Fletchers Way. E Gos —2D **24**
Fletcher Way. E Gos —2D **24**
Forest Clo. Lou —2G **11**
Forest Dri. Sile —3E **17**
Foresters Row. E Gos —2D **24**
Forest Rd. Lou —4E **11**
Forest Rd. Quor —2C **14**
Forest Rd. Wood —3A **14**
Forest Rd. Wood E —4B **14**
Forest St. Shep —4E **9**
Forman Rd. Shep —3D **8**
Forsyth Clo. Lou —5B **4**
Fort Rd. Mount —6H **15**
Fosse Way. Sys —6H **23**
Foundry La. Sys —6H **23**
Fowke St. Roth —3B **22**
Foxcote Dri. Lou —3A **10**
Fox Covert. Lou —5H **5**
Foxglove Clo. E Gos —2E **25**
Fox Hollow. E Gos —1D **24**
Francis Dri. Lou —5C **4**
Frederick Clo. Quen —3E **25**

Frederick St. Lou —2G **11**
Freehold St. Lou —1A **12**
Freehold St. Quor —1F **15**
Freehold St. Shep —2E **9**
Freeman's Way. E Gos —1E **25**
Freeman Way. Quor —6D **12**
Furlongs Clo. Sys —6C **24**
Furrow Clo. Roth —2A **22**

Gaddesby La. Rear —6G **19**
Gallico Clo. Lou —6D **4**
Gamble Way. Quor —6D **12**
Gardner Clo. Lou —5C **4**
Garendon Av. Hath —3A **4**
Garendon Clo. Shep —2E **9**
Garendon Grn. Lou —2D **10**
Garendon Rd. Lou —1D **10**
Garendon Rd. Shep —2D **8**
Garland. Roth —2A **22**
Garton Rd. Lou —2H **11**
Gascoigne Av. Quen —4E **25**
Gavin Dri. Lou —5D **4**
Gelders Hall Ind. Est. Shep
 —4C **8**
Gelders Hall Rd. Shep —3C **8**
George Deacon Ct. Lou —2G **11**
 (off Ashby Rd.)
George St. Lou —1F **11**
George Toon Ct. Sys —5A **24**
George Yd. Lou —1H **11**
Gibson Rd. Sile —3F **17**
Giles Clo. Quor —2F **15**
Gipsy La. Roth —1G **21**
Gisborough Way. Lou —5A **4**
Gladstone Av. Lou —6G **5**
Gladstone St. Hath —2A **4**
Gladstone St. Lou —6H **5**
Glamis Clo. Mount —1H **21**
Glebe Clo. Mount —5H **15**
Glebe Rd. Quen —4E **25**
Glebe St. Lou —6A **6**
Glebe Way. Sys —5G **23**
Glenfields. Shep —2C **8**
Glenmore Av. Shep —1C **8**
Gloucester Av. Sys —5C **24**
Golden Sq. Hath —3H **3**
Golding Clo. Lou —5C **4**
Goode's Av. Sys —6A **24**
Goode's La. Sys —6A **24**
Gordon Rd. Lou —5H **5**
Gorse La. Sys —6H **23**
Gracedieu Rd. Lou —2C **10**
Grafton Rd. Lou —5E **5**
Graham Rise. Lou —5D **4**
Granby St. Lou —1G **11**
Grange Av. Rear —1F **25**
Grangefields Dri. Roth —3B **22**
Grange La. Mount —1H **21**
Grange Rd. Shep —2C **8**
Grange St. Lou —6G **5**
Granite Way. Mount —4G **15**
Granville St. Lou —1G **11**
Grasmere Clo. Bar S —5H **13**
Grasmere Rd. Lou —6F **11**
Grassholme Dri. Lou —3A **10**
Gray St. Lou —3H **11**
Gt. Central La. Lou —2A **12**
Grebe Clo. Bar S —5H **13**
Greedon Rise. Sile —3F **17**
Greenfell Hall. Lou —1E **11**
Greenhill. Hath —2A **4**
Green Hill Rise. Hath —1A **4**

Greenhouse La. Lou —1G **11**
Green La. Sea —1A **18**
Green La. Clo. Sea —1A **18**
Greensward. E Gos —1E **25**
Green, The. Hath —2A **4**
Green, The. Long W —1E **3**
Green, The. Mount —5A **16**
Green, The. Sys —5B **24**
Green, The. Thrus —3F **19**
Greenway Clo. Roth —3A **22**
Gregory St. Lou —2H **11**
Griffin Clo. Shep —2C **8**
Griggs Rd. Lou —5H **11**
Grove La. Bar S —6H **13**
Grove Rd. Lou —2E **11**
Grove, The. Lou —1E **11**
Guildford Way. Lou —5C **10**

Haddon Clo. Sys —6H **23**
Hailey Av. Lou —6C **4**
Halfcroft, The. Sys —5A **24**
Halford St. Sys —6A **24**
Hallamford Rd. Shep —4B **2**
Hall Croft. Shep —1D **8**
Hall Dri. Bur W —5G **7**
Hall Farm Clo. Quen —4F **25**
Hallfields La. Roth —3A **22**
Hall Leys. Quor —2E **15**
Halstead Rd. Mount —6G **15**
Hambledon Cres. Lou —5F **11**
Hanford Way. Lou —6H **5**
Hanover Ct. Lou —6D **4**
Hanover Dri. Sile —4F **17**
Harcourt Clo. Sys —5A **24**
Hardwick Cres. Sys —6H **23**
Hardwick Dri. Lou —1C **10**
Harlech Clo. Lou —6E **5**
Harrington Clo. Quor —1E **15**
Harrington Rd. Shep —2E **9**
Harrisons Row. Sys —5B **24**
Harvesters Corner. E Gos
 —2E **25**
Hastings Rd. Wood E —6B **14**
Hastings St. Lou —1G **11**
Hathern Dri. Lou & Hath —5H **3**
Hathern Rd. Long W —1F **3**
Hathern Rd. Shep —6E **3**
Havelock St. Lou —1F **11**
Hawcliffe Rd. Mount —4G **15**
Hawthorne Av. Hath —1H **3**
Hawthorn Rd. Mount —6A **16**
Haybrooke Rd. Sile —3F **17**
Haydon Rd. Lou —1E **11**
Hayhill La. Bar S —1B **16**
Hayward Av. Lou —3A **12**
Hazel Rd. Lou —5G **11**
Hazlerigg Hall. Lou —2E **11**
Headland, The. E Gos —1E **25**
Heath Av. Sys —6H **23**
Heathcote Dri. Sile —3F **17**
Heathcote St. Lou —1G **11**
Herbert St. Lou —6H **5**
Hermitage Rd. Lou —3B **10**
Heron Clo. Mount —5B **16**
Heron Rd. Bar S —5H **13**
Heron's Way. E Gos —1E **25**
Heron Way. Sys —5H **23**
Herrick Rd. Lou —3G **11**
Herrick Rd. Wood E —4B **14**
Herriot Way. Lou —6D **4**
Hickling Ct. Lou —1F **11**
Hickling Dri. Sile —3F **17**

Highbridge. Sile —4E **17**
Highfields. Bar S —5H **13**
Highfields Clo. Shep —6E **3**
Highfields Dri. Lou —3D **10**
Highfields Rd. Mount —6H **15**
Highgate Rd. Sile —4F **17**
High Meadow. Hath —2A **4**
High St. Barrow-upon-Soar,
Bar S —6G **13**
High St. Loughborough, Lou
—1H **11**
High St. Quorndon, Quor
—1D **14**
High St. Sileby, Sile —4E **17**
High St. Syston, Sys —5A **24**
Hill Rise. Wood E —5B **14**
Hill Top Rd. Lou —5E **11**
Hobbs Wick. Sile —4E **17**
Hoby Rd. Thrus —3F **19**
Hodson Clo. Lou —3H **11**
Holbein Clo. Lou —1A **12**
Holbourne Clo. Bar S —6H **13**
Hollybush Clo. Sys —5H **23**
Hollytree Clo. Hot —1G **7**
Hollytree Clo. Lou —6G **11**
Holmdale Rd. Sys —6A **24**
Holmfield Av. Lou —5F **5**
Holt Dri. Lou —3F **11**
Holt Rise. Shep —4E **9**
Holywell Clo. Lou —4C **10**
Holywell Way. Lou —3C **10**
Homefield La. Roth —3B **22**
Homefield Rd. Sile —3E **17**
Homestead Clo. Costn —1F **23**
Homestead, The. Mount
—4H **15**
Homeway Clo. Shep —2E **9**
Hornbeam Clo. Lou —6G **11**
Hornecroft. Roth —3A **22**
Hospital Way. Lou —1E **11**
Howard Clo. Lou —6C **4**
Howard St. Lou —6H **5**
Howden Clo. Lou —2B **10**
Howe La. Roth —3A **22**
Howe Rd. Lou —4H **11**
Hudson Rd. Sile —3E **17**
Hudson St. Lou —1A **12**
Humble La. Costn —1F **23**
Hume St. Lou —1A **12**
Hungarton Dri. Sys —6C **24**
Huntingdon Ct. Lou —1G **11**
Huntington Clo. Bur W —5G **7**
Huntsmans Clo. Quor —1F **15**
Huntsman's Dale. E Gos
—1D **24**
Hurstwood Rd. Lou —2B **10**
Huston Clo. Bar S —1A **16**
Huston Ct. Lou —2G **11**

Iliffes Clo. Bar S —5H **13**
Ingleberry Rd. Shep —4E **9**
Inleys, The. Shep —2F **9**
Iona Rd. Sys —5H **23**
Iris Clo. Mount —5B **16**
Irwin Av. Lou —5C **4**
Iveshead La. Shep —5C **8**
Iveshead Rd. Shep —6C **8**

James Av. Lou —5C **4**
Japonica Clo. Lou —6G **11**
Jasmine Clo. Lou —6G **11**

Jetcott Av. Lou —6G **11**
John Phillips Ct. Lou —1E **11**
Johns Av. Mount —1A **22**
John's Lee Clo. Lou —4F **11**
Jolly Farmers La. Shep —5C **8**
Jubilee Av. Sile —2F **17**
Jubilee Clo. Lou —5G **5**
Judges St. Lou —2A **12**
Juniper Way. Lou —6G **11**

Keats Way. Lou —6D **4**
Keble Dri. Sys —6B **24**
Keepers' Croft. E Gos —2E **25**
Kelcey Rd. Quor —6D **12**
Kendal Rd. Sile —5F **17**
Kenilworth Av. Lou —1C **10**
Kensington Av. Lou —6C **4**
Kernan Dri. Lou —4F **5**
Kestrel Clo. Sys —5H **23**
Keswick Av. Lou —4D **10**
Kilbourne Clo. Sile —5E **17**
Kinchley La. Roth —6E **15**
King Edward Rd. Lou —2A **12**
Kingfisher Clo. Bar S —5H **13**
Kingfisher Clo. Mount —5B **16**
Kingfisher Clo. Sys —5H **23**
Kingfisher Rd. Mount —6B **16**
Kingfisher Way. Lou —3G **11**
King George Av. Lou —3B **12**
King George Rd. Lou —3B **12**
Kings Av. Lou —5F **5**
King's Rd. Shep —3D **8**
King St. Lou —2A **12**
King St. Sea —1A **18**
King St. Sile —4E **17**
Kingswood Av. Lou —5B **4**
Kinross Cres. Lou —6D **4**
Kirby Clo. Mount —1H **21**
Kirkhill. Shep —1E **9**
Kirkstone Dri. Lou —4C **10**
Knights Cres. Roth —3A **22**
Knightthorpe Ct. Lou —6D **4**
Knightthorpe Rd. Lou —1D **10**
Knipton Dri. Lou —2C **10**

Laburnum Clo. Hath —2A **4**
Lacey Ct. Shep —2D **8**
Ladybower Rd. Lou —3B **10**
Lambert Av. Shep —2D **8**
Lamport Clo. Lou —1C **10**
Lanesborough Ct. Lou —3G **11**
Lanesborough Dri. Thurc
—6F **21**
Lanes Clo. Sile —3F **17**
Laneshaw Av. Lou —3B **10**
Langdale Av. Lou —4D **10**
Lansdowne Av. Shep —6E **3**
Lansdowne Dri. Lou —4G **11**
Lansdowne Rd. Shep —6D **2**
Lant, The. Shep —1E **9**
Latimer Rd. Crop —6D **20**
Laurel Clo. Mount —5A **16**
Laurel Rd. Lou —6G **11**
Lawrence Way. Lou —4C **4**
Leake La. Stan S —2A **6**
Leckhampton Rd. Lou —1C **10**
Leconfield Rd. Lou —6C **10**
Ledbury Rd. Lou —6F **11**
Leicester La. Swit —4B **20**
Leicester Rd. Lou & LE12
—2H **11**

Leicester Rd. Quor —2E **15**
Leicester Rd. Shep —2E **9**
Leicester Rd. Thurc —6E **21**
Leighton Av. Lou —2B **10**
Lemontree Av. Lou —6G **11**
Lemyngton St. Lou —1H **11**
Leopold St. Lou —1F **11**
Leslie Clo. Lou —5D **4**
Lewis Rd. Lou —6D **4**
Leys, The. E Gos —1E **25**
Leys, The. Hath —3A **4**
Lilac Clo. Lou —6G **11**
Lilleshall Way. Lou —6B **4**
Lime Av. Lou —2A **12**
Lime Clo. Sys —6B **24**
Limehurst Av. Lou —6G **5**
Lincoln Dri. Sys —6C **24**
Linden Gro. Mount —6A **16**
Linden Rd. Lou —6G **5**
Lindisfarne Clo. Lou —5A **4**
Lindisfarne Dri. Lou —5A **4**
Lindisfarne Rd. Sys —6H **23**
Lindum Clo. Sys —6H **23**
Linford Rd. Lou —5E **11**
Ling Av. Lou —5A **12**
Ling Dale. E Gos —2E **25**
Lingdale Clo. Lou —4H **11**
Lingdale Lodge. E Gos —2E **25**
Ling Rd. Lou —4H **11**
Linkfield Av. Mount —6A **16**
Linkfield Rd. Mount —6A **16**
Link Rd. Quen —4D **24**
Linley Av. Shep —3E **9**
Lisle St. Lou —6G **5**
Lit. Church La. Sile —4E **17**
Lit. Haw La. Shep —2C **8**
Lit. Moor La. Lou —2A **12**
Lodge Clo. Sys —5C **24**
Longcliffe Gdns. Nan —6A **10**
Longcliffe Rd. Shep —2C **8**
Long Clo. Quor —6D **12**
Long Furlong. Mount —1H **21**
Long Furrow. E Gos —2D **24**
Lorrimer Way. Lou —6C **4**
Loughborough Rd. Bur W
—5G **7**
Loughborough Rd. Cotes
—5D **6**
Loughborough Rd. Hath —2A **4**
Loughborough Rd. Lou & Pres
—5D **6**
Loughborough Rd. Mount
—3G **15**
Loughborough Rd. Quor
—5B **12**
Loughborough Rd. Shep —1E **9**
Lovett Ct. Bar S —1A **16**
Lwr. Cambridge St. Lou —6H **5**
Lwr. Church St. Sys —5B **24**
Lwr. Gladstone St. Lou —6H **5**
Lower Grn. Lou —5D **10**
Loweswater Clo. Bar S —4G **13**
Loweswater Dri. Lou —4C **10**
Lowther Way. Lou —4H **11**
Ludlow Clo. Lou —5C **10**
Ludlow Pl. Shep —3C **8**
Lyall Clo. Lou —5D **4**

Macaulay Rd. Roth —3A **22**
McCarthy Rd. Shep —1C **8**
Maclean Av. Lou —5C **4**
Magnolia Av. Lou —6G **11**

Maiden St. Sys —6H **23**
Main St. Costn —1E **23**
Main St. Nor S —1D **4**
Main St. Quen —4F **25**
Main St. Rat W —6B **18**
Main St. Stan S —2A **6**
Main St. Swit —2A **20**
Main St. Wood E —4B **14**
Maitland Av. Mount —6A **16**
Mallard Dri. Sys —5H **23**
Mallard Rd. Bar S —5H **13**
Mallard Rd. Mount —5B **16**
Malvern Av. Shep —3E **9**
Manor Dri. Lou —5H **11**
Manor Dri. Sile —5E **17**
Manor Gdns. Shep —1D **8**
Manor Rd. Lou —6H **11**
Mansfield Av. Quor —1E **15**
Mansfield St. Quor —1E **15**
Maple Rd. Lou —5H **11**
Maple Rd. N. Lou —5H **11**
Maple Rd. S. Lou —6H **11**
Maplewell Rd. Wood E —6A **14**
Mardale Way. Lou —5D **10**
Marigold La. Mount —5B **16**
Market Pl. Lou —1H **11**
Market Pl. Mount —4A **16**
Market Pl. Shep —1D **8**
Market St. Lou —1G **11**
Marsden Av. Quen —4D **24**
Marshall Av. Sile —3F **17**
Marsh Rd. Mount —6A **16**
Martin Av. Bar S —6H **13**
Martin Av. Mount —6H **15**
Martindale Clo. Lou —4D **10**
Martin Dri. Sys —5G **23**
Maxwell Dri. Lou —5B **4**
Mayfield Dri. Lou —3G **11**
Mayo Clo. Lou —6F **11**
May Tree La. Wood —3A **14**
Meadow Av. Lou —5H **5**
Meadow Clo. Bar S —5H **13**
Meadow La. Lou & Stan S
—6H **5**
Meadow La. Sys —5G **23**
Meadow Rd. Mount —1H **21**
Meadow Rd. Wood E —5C **14**
Meadows, The. E Gos —1E **25**
Meadows, The. Shep —3C **8**
Meeting St. Quor —2D **14**
Melbreak Av. Lou —5E **11**
Melton Rd. Bar S —6H **13**
Melton Rd. Bur W —5H **7**
Melton Rd. Sys —6A **24**
Melville Clo. Lou —5B **4**
Mendip Clo. Shep —2E **9**
Mercer's Way. E Gos —2E **25**
Merchants Comn. E Gos
—2E **25**
Mere Clo. Mount —1A **22**
Mere La. Quen —4F **25**
Merton Av. Sys —6B **24**
Messenger Clo. Lou —4E **5**
Meynell Rd. Quor —6F **13**
(in two parts)
Michael Clo. Quen —4E **25**
Middle Av. Lou —5F **5**
Middlefield Rd. Costn —1F **23**
Middle Orchard. Sile —6E **17**
Middleton Pl. Lou —3H **11**
Mildenhall Rd. Lou —1C **10**
Mill Clo. Shep —6E **3**
Millers Clo. Sys —6A **24**

Mill La. Bar S —6H **13**
Mill La. Lou —1G **11**
(Market St.)
Mill La. Lou —6A **6**
(Nottingham Rd.)
Mill La. Sile —5C **16**
Mill La. Sys —4H **23**
Mill Rd. Rear —6F **19**
Mill Rd. Thurc —6F **21**
Mill Rd. Wood E —5B **14**
Mills, The. Quor —2E **15**
Millstone La. Sys —4C **24**
Mills Yd. Lou —2H **11**
Milner Clo. Sile —5E **17**
Milton St. Lou —5E **5**
Minstrels Wlk. E Gos —2D **24**
Mitchell Dri. Lou —5B **4**
Moat Rd. Lou —5E **11**
Model Farm Clo. Lou —4E **11**
Moira St. Lou —2H **11**
Molyneux Dri. Sile —6F **17**
Monarch Way. Lou —5G **5**
Monsarrat Way. Lou —5D **4**
Montague Av. Sys —6B **24**
Montague Dri. Lou —5C **10**
Montsoreau Way. Mount
—1H **21**
Moorfield Pl. Shep —1D **8**
Moorland Rd. Sys —5G **23**
Moor La. Lou —1H **11**
(in two parts)
Moreton Dale. Sile —3F **17**
Morley La. Shep —4C **8**
Morley St. Lou —6A **6**
Morris Clo. Lou —1A **12**
Morris Hall. Lou —1E **11**
Mortimer Way. Lou —5B **4**
Moscow La. Shep —4C **8**
Mostyn Av. Sys —5C **24**
Mountfields Dri. Lou —3E **11**
Mt. Grace Rd. Lou —6B **4**
Mountsorrel La. Mount & Roth
—1A **22**
Mountsorrel La. Sile —4B **16**
Mowbray Dri. Sys —5C **24**
Muckle Ga. La. Sea —1A **18**
Mumford Hall. Lou —2D **12**
Mundy Clo. Bur W —5G **7**
Murdoch Rise. Lou —5D **4**

Nanhill Dri. Wood E —6C **14**
Nanpantan Rd. Nan & Lou
—6H **9**
Narrow La. Hath —2A **4**
Naseby Dri. Lou —3A **10**
Navigation Way. Lou —6G **5**
Navins, The. Mount —4H **15**
Naylor Av. Lou —3B **12**
Naylor Rd. Sys —4C **24**
Necton St. Lou —6A **24**
Nelson Clo. Shep —1F **9**
Nelson St. Sys —6B **24**
Neville Clo. Shep —1D **8**
Newark Clo. Shep —2B **8**
New Ashby Rd. Lou —4G **9**
New Av. Rear —6G **19**
Newbold Clo. Sile —3F **17**
Newbon Clo. Lou —1E **11**
New King St. Lou —2A **12**
Newlands Av. Shep —3E **9**
New St. Bar S —6H **13**
New St. Lou —2G **11**

New St. Quen —4E **25**
Newton Clo. Bar S —5H **13**
Newton Clo. Lou —5D **4**
New Wlk. Shep —1D **8**
New Wlks. Lou —3A **12**
New Zealand La. Quen —3C **24**
Nicolson Rd. Lou —5C **10**
Nightingale Av. Hath —2B **4**
Nook Clo. Shep —3E **9**
Normanton La. Stan S —2H **5**
Northage Clo. Quor —3F **15**
Northfields. Sys —5B **24**
N. Hill Clo. Sile —3G **17**
(in two parts)
North Rd. Lou —5H **5**
North St. Bar S —5H **13**
North St. Roth —3A **22**
North St. Sys —5A **24**
Northwood Dri. Shep —5E **3**
Norwich Clo. Shep —3C **8**
Nottingham Rd. Bar S —5H **13**
Nottingham Rd. Lou & LE12
—1H **11**
Nursery Clo. Quen —4E **25**
Nursery Clo. Shep —5E **3**
Nursery End. Lou —5D **10**
Nursery Gro. Bar S —4H **13**
Nursery La. Quor —1E **15**
Nutkin Clo. Lou —3F **11**

Oakham Clo. Lou —5E **5**
Oakhurst Ct. Lou —1C **10**
Oaklands Av. Lou —3F **11**
Oakley Av. Shep —1D **8**
Oakley Clo. Shep —6D **2**
Oakley Dri. Long W —1D **2**
Oakley Dri. Lou —4F **11**
Oakley Estates. Shep —6D **2**
Oakley Rd. Shep —6D **2**
Oakwood Dri. Lou —4B **10**
Old Ashby Rd. Lou —3A **10**
Old Forge Clo. Hath —2A **4**
Old Gate Rd. Thrus —1E **19**
Old Parsonage La. Hot —2G **7**
Old Station Clo. Shep —3D **8**
Old Way. Hath —2A **4**
Oliver Rd. Lou —3H **11**
One Barrow La. Char —6A **8**
Orchard Est. Quor —1D **14**
Orchard St. Lou —1G **11**
Orchard, The. Sea —1A **18**
Orchard View. Mount —1A **22**
Orchard Way. Sys —6C **24**
Oriel Dri. Sys —6B **24**
Orwell Clo. Lou —5D **4**
Osborne Rd. Lou —5C **4**
Osiers, The. Lou —6G **11**
Osiers, The. Mount —6G **15**
Osterley Clo. Lou —1C **10**
Outwoods Av. Lou —4F **11**
Outwoods Dri. Lou —3F **11**
Outwoods Rd. Lou —5F **11**
Oxburgh Clo. Lou —6C **4**
Oxford Ct. Sys —5C **24**
Oxford St. Lou —1F **11**
Oxford St. Shep —3D **8**
Oxford St. Sys —5C **24**
Oxley Clo. Shep —2C **8**

Packe St. Lou —1G **11**
Packhorse La. Lou —2H **11**

Paddock Clo. Quor —2E **15**
Paddock Clo. Roth —4A **22**
Paddock, The. Shep —2D **8**
Paddock View. Sys —6H **23**
Paget St. Lou —1F **11**
Palma Pk. Home Est. Lou
—6D **4**
Palmer Av. Lou —6F **5**
Pantain Rd. Lou —5E **11**
Parade, The. Shep —3C **8**
Park Av. Lou —4H **11**
Park Av. Shep —3E **9**
Park Clo. Shep —1D **8**
Park Ct. Lou —3H **11**
Parkers Fields. Quor —6E **13**
Park Hill La. Sea —2B **18**
Parklands Dri. Lou —5G **11**
Park Rise. Shep —2D **8**
Park Rd. Lou —6G **11**
Park Rd. Sile —3E **17**
Parkstone Rd. Sys —4B **24**
Park St. Lou —2H **11**
Parsons Dri. Sile —3G **17**
Partridge Clo. Sys —5H **23**
Pasture La. Hath —2A **4**
Pastures, The. Bar S —1A **16**
Pastures, The. Sys —6G **23**
Paterson Dri. Wood E —5B **14**
Paterson Pl. Shep —6D **2**
Patterdale Dri. Lou —4C **10**
Peartree Av. Shep —2F **9**
Pear Tree La. Lou —5A **4**
Peashill Clo. Sile —4G **17**
Pedlars Way. E Gos —2D **24**
Peel Dri. Lou —1A **12**
Peggs La. Quen —4F **25**
Pell Clo. Bar S —5H **13**
Pembroke Av. Sys —6B **24**
Pennine Clo. Shep —3E **9**
Penrith Av. Shep —3B **8**
Pentland Av. Shep —3F **9**
Pepper Dri. Quor —6D **12**
Peppers Clo. Mount —4H **15**
Perry Clo. Wood E —4B **14**
Perry Gro. Lou —4A **12**
Petworth Dri. Lou —6C **4**
Pevensey Rd. Lou —5E **5**
Phoenix Dri. Sile —5F **17**
Pick St. Shep —1D **8**
Pine Clo. Lou —6G **11**
Pine Dri. Sys —6B **24**
Pinfold Gdns. Lou —1A **12**
Pinfold Ga. Lou —1H **11**
Pinfold Jetty. Lou —1H **11**
Pingle, The. Quor —2C **14**
Piper Clo. Lou —4F **11**
Piper Clo. Shep —5E **3**
Piper Dri. Long W —1E **3**
Pitsford Dri. Lou —3A **10**
Plain Ga. Roth —1G **11**
Platts La. Costn —2E **23**
Pleasant Clo. Lou —1G **11**
Plough Clo. Mount —1H **21**
Ploughmans Dri. Shep —6E **3**
Ploughmans' Lea. E Gos
—2D **24**
Plumtree Clo. Lou —5F **5**
Plumtree Way. Sys —6B **24**
Pochin Way. Sile —3F **17**
Pocket End. Lou —5E **11**
Polden Clo. Shep —3E **9**
Pond St. Sea —2A **18**
Poplar Rd. Lou —5H **11**

Porlock Clo. Shep —3E **9**
Poulteney Dri. Quor —1D **14**
Prestbury Rd. Lou —1B **10**
Prestwold La. Pres —2G **7**
Prevost Gdns. Quor —6E **13**
Primrose Way. Quen —3E **25**
Princess St. Lou —2H **11**
Prince William Rd. Lou —5G **5**
Priory Clo. Sys —6H **23**
Priory Rd. Lou —5E **11**
Proctors Pk. Rd. Bar S —6G **13**
Proctors Pleasure Pk. Bar S
—6G **13**
Pryor Rd. Sile —3F **17**
Pudding Bag La. Shep —5B **8**
Pulteney Av. Lou —5H **11**
Pulteney Rd. Lou —5H **11**
Purbeck Av. Shep —2F **9**
Purley Rise. Shep —3E **9**
Pytchley Dri. Lou —5F **11**

Quaker Rd. Sile —6E **17**
Quantock Rise. Shep —3E **9**
Queen's Rd. Lou —6A **6**
Queen St. Lou —2A **12**
Queen St. Shep —1E **9**
Quenby Cres. Sys —6C **24**
Queniborough Ind. Est. Quen
—4D **25**
Queniborough Rd. Quen
—4E **25**
Queniborough Rd. Sys —6D **24**
Quorn Clo. Lou —3A **12**
Quorndon-Mountsorrel By-Pass.
Quor & Mount —6C **12**

Radmoor Rd. Lou —2F **11**
Radnor Dri. Shep —6D **2**
Railway Ter. Lou —6A **6**
Ratcliffe Rd. Lou —6H **5**
Ratcliffe Rd. Sile & Rat W
—4F **17**
Ratcliffe Rd. Thrus —3F **19**
Ravensthorpe Dri. Lou —2B **10**
Rawlins Clo. Wood E —5C **14**
Raymond Av. Lou —5D **4**
Raynham Dri. Lou —6C **4**
Rearsby Rd. Quen —3E **25**
Rearsby Rd. Thrus —3F **19**
Rectory Pl. Lou —6H **5**
Rectory Rd. Lou —6H **5**
Rectory Rd. Wan & LE4
—6D **22**
Redmires Clo. Lou —2B **10**
Redwood Rd. Lou —6G **11**
Regent Ct. Lou —6G **5**
Regent St. Lou —1G **11**
Regent St. Thrus —3F **19**
Rempstone Rd. Hot —1G **7**
Rempstone Rd. Shep —4A **2**
Rendell St. Lou —6H **5**
(in two parts)
Renning End. Mount —1A **22**
Reservoir Rd. Crop —6B **20**
Retreat, The. Bar S —1H **15**
Revell Clo. Quor —1F **15**
Ribble Dri. Bar S —1H **15**
Ridgemere Clo. Sys —5D **24**
Ridgemere La. Quen —6E **25**
Ridgeway, The. Roth —4F **21**
Ridings, The. Quen —4E **25**

Ridings, The. Roth —2E **21**
Ring Fence. Shep —3D **8**
Ringway, The. Quen —3E **25**
Ringwood Rd. Shep —6D **2**
Rise, The. Roth —3C **22**
Riverview. Bar S —1A **16**
Rivington Dri. Lou —3B **10**
Rochester Clo. Mount —1H **21**
Rockhill Dri. Mount —1H **21**
Rockingham Clo. Shep —3C **8**
Rockingham Rd. Lou —5E **5**
Rockingham Rd. Mount
—1H **21**
Romans, The. Mount —6H **15**
Romway Clo. Shep —2E **9**
Roecliffe Rd. Wood E & Crop
—5A **20**
Ronald West Ct. Lou —4D **10**
Roods, The. Roth —3A **22**
Rookery, The. Bar S —5G **13**
Rosebery St. Lou —1F **11**
Rosehill. Lou —1C **10**
Rosslyn Av. Mount —6G **15**
Rothley Rd. Mount —5A **16**
Roughford Clo. Lou —6B **4**
Roundhill Clo. Sys —6H **23**
Roundhill Way. Lou —2B **10**
Rowan Av. Hath —1A **4**
Rowbank Way. Lou —2B **10**
Rowena Ct. Mount —1A **22**
Royal Way. Lou —5G **5**
Royce Hall. Lou —3D **10**
Roydale Clo. Lou —5E **5**
Royland Rd. Lou —2H **11**
Rubicon Clo. Mount —6B **16**
Rudyard Clo. Lou —3B **10**
Rufford Clo. Lou —6B **4**
Rumsey Clo. Quor —1C **14**
Rupert Brooke Rd. Lou —1D **10**
Rupert Cres. Quen —3E **25**
Rupert Law Clo. Quor —6D **12**
Rushes, The. Lou —1G **11**
Rushey La. Roth —5F **15**
Ruskin Av. Sys —6C **24**
Russ Clo. Quor —6D **12**
Russell St. Lou —1A **12**
Rutherford Hall. Lou —2D **10**
Rutland Hall. Lou —2E **11**
Rutland St. Lou —2A **12**
Rydal Av. Lou —4D **10**

Saddlers' Clo. E Gos —2D **24**
St Aidan's Av. Sys —6H **23**
St Andrews Clo. Bur W —5H **7**
St Bernard's Clo. Shep —2D **8**
St Botolph Rd. Shep —2D **8**
St Columba Way. Sys —5H **23**
St Gregorys Dri. Sile —4F **17**
St James Rd. Shep —2D **8**
St John's Av. Sys —6C **24**
St Joseph Clo. Hot —2H **7**
St Leonards Clo. Bur W —5H **7**
St Marys Clo. Bur W —5H **7**
St Mary's Clo. Lou —1F **11**
St Mary's Rd. Sile —3E **17**
St Olaves Clo. Lou —6B **4**
St Pauls Ct. Sys —5A **24**
St Paul's Dri. Sys —6A **24**
St Peter's Av. Hath —2A **4**
St Peter's Ct. Sys —5B **24**
St Peter's St. Sys —6A **24**
St Phillips Rd. Bur W —5H **7**

St Winefride Rd. Shep —2D **8**
Salisbury St. Lou —1A **12**
Salmon M. Shep —1D **8**
Sandalwood Rd. Lou —4E **11**
Sanders Rd. Quor —1D **14**
Sandford Rd. Sys —6A **24**
Sandham Bri. Rd. Crop —6D **20**
Sandhills, The. Quor —1C **14**
Sandhole La. Shep —4A **8**
Sandringham Dri. Lou —6D **4**
Sandringham Rise. Shep —3B **8**
Sarson St. Quor —1D **14**
Schofield Rd. Lou —2C **10**
School La. Quen —4F **25**
School La. Quor —2E **15**
School St. Lou —1H **11**
School St. Roth —3B **22**
School St. Sys —5B **24**
Seagrave Rd. Sile —4E **17**
Seagrave Rd. Thrus —1C **18**
Seals Clo. Bur W —5H **7**
Sedgefield Dri. Sys —6G **23**
Selbourne Ct. Lou —2A **12**
Selbourne St. Lou —1A **12**
Selvester Dri. Quor —2F **15**
Seton Clo. Lou —5C **4**
Seward St. Lou —2G **11**
Seymour Clo. Lou —6B **4**
Seymour Rd. Bur W —5G **7**
Shakespeare St. Lou —1H **11**
Sharpley Rd. Lou —3B **10**
Sheepcote. Roth —2A **22**
Sheldon Clo. Lou —5B **4**
Shelley St. Lou —6D **4**
Shelthorpe Av. Lou —4H **11**
Shelthorpe Ho. Lou —4H **11**
Shelthorpe Rd. Lou —4H **11**
Shepherds Clo. Lou —4D **10**
Shepherds Clo. Shep —6E **3**
Shepherd's Wlk. E Gos —2D **24**
Shepshed Rd. Hath —4F **3**
Sherrard Dri. Sile —6E **17**
Shirley Dri. Sys —4B **24**
Shirreffs Clo. Bar S —5H **13**
Sileby Rd. Bar S —6H **13**
Sileby Rd. Mount —4A **16**
Sileby Rd. Ind. Est. Sile
—4E **17**
Silver Birches. Quor —1D **14**
Silverbirch Way. E Gos —1E **25**
Silverton Rd. Lou —5F **11**
Sir Robert Martin Ct. Lou
—6D **4**
Skevington Av. Lou —2E **11**
Skylark Av. Mount —5B **16**
Slash La. Bar S —2B **16**
Smithy La. Long W —1C **2**
Smithy Way. Shep —1E **9**
Snell's Nook La. Nan —4A **10**
Snowdon Clo. Shep —3E **9**
Soarbank Way. Lou —4E **5**
Soar La. Nor S —1D **4**
Soar Rd. Quor —1F **15**
Somerset Clo. Bur W —5G **7**
Sorrel Ct. Mount —5A **16**
S. Croxton Rd. Quen —4G **25**
Southdown Rd. Lou —6G **11**
Southfield Av. Sys —6B **24**
Southfield Rd. Lou —2H **11**
South St. Bar S —6H **13**
South St. Lou —2H **11**
Sowters La. Bur W —5H **7**
Sparrow Hill. Lou —1H **11**

Speeds Pingle. Lou —1G **11**
Speedwell Rd. Mount —5B **16**
Spinney Clo. Sys —6G **23**
Spinney Dri. Quor —2D **14**
Spinney Hill Dri. Lou —3D **10**
Spring Clo. Shep —3E **9**
Springfield Clo. Bur W —5G **7**
Springfield Clo. Lou —5E **11**
Springfield Rd. Shep —2D **8**
Springfield Rd. Sile —3E **17**
Spring La. Long W —1F **3**
Spring La. Shep —3D **8**
Spruce Av. Lou —6F **11**
Squires Ride. E Gos —1D **24**
Squirrel's Corner. E Gos
—1E **25**
Squirrel Way. Lou —3F **11**
Stamford Dri. Crop —6D **20**
Stanage Rd. Sile —3G **17**
Stanford Hill. Lou —5H **5**
Stanford La. Cotes —3B **6**
Stanford Rd. Nor S —1E **5**
Stanley St. Lou —3H **11**
Station Av. Lou —6F **5**
Station Rd. Crop —6C **20**
Station Rd. Quor —1E **15**
Station Rd. Rear —4G **19**
Station Rd. Sys —6A **24**
Station St. Lou —1F **11**
Staveley Clo. Sile —5F **17**
Staveley Ct. Lou —6H **5**
Steeple Row. Lou —1H **11**
Stewart Dri. Lou —6C **4**
Stiles, The. Sys —5B **24**
(in two parts)
Stirling Av. Lou —6D **4**
Stirling Clo. Mount —1G **21**
Stirling Clo. Quor —6D **12**
Stonebow Clo. Lou —5B **4**
Stonebow Wlk. Lou —5A **4**
Stonehurst La. Nor S —1D **4**
Stoop La. Quor —1E **15**
Storer Clo. Sile —4F **17**
Storer Rd. Lou —1F **11**
Strachan Clo. Mount —6A **16**
Strancliffe La. Bar S —4G **13**
Strollers Way. E Gos —2D **24**
Sullington Rd. Shep —3D **8**
Sullivan Way. Lou —4F **5**
Summerpool Rd. Lou —4F **5**
Sunnyhill Rd. Lou —4F **11**
Sutton Clo. Quor —2D **14**
Swallow Clo. Sys —5G **23**
Swallows Dale. E Gos —1E **25**
Swallow Wlk. Hath —2A **4**
Swan Clo. Bar S —5H **13**
Swan Clo. Mount —5B **16**
Swan St. Lou —1H **11**
Swan St. Sea —1A **18**
Swan St. Sile —4E **17**
Swan Way. Sys —5G **23**
Swift Clo. Sys —5H **23**
Swinfield Rd. Quor —1E **15**
Swingbridge Rd. Lou —5F **5**
Swithland Clo. Lou —6C **4**
Swithland Ct. Wood E —6C **14**
Swithland La. Roth —3F **21**
Swithland Rd. Swit —5C **20**
Sycamore Way. Lou —6G **11**
Syston By-Pass. Sys —4G **23**
Syston Northern By-Pass. Sys
—3A **24**
Syston Rd. Costn —2D **22**

Syston Rd. Quen —3D **24**
Sywell Av. Lou —2C **10**

Tailors Link. E Gos —2D **24**
Tamworth Clo. Shep —3B **8**
Tanners La. Hath —2A **4**
Tatmarsh. Lou —6H **5**
Taylor Clo. Sys —6A **24**
Teal Way. Sys —5G **23**
Telford Hall. Lou —3D **10**
Templar Way. Roth —3H **21**
Temple Clo. Shep —4E **9**
Tennyson Rd. Lou —1D **10**
Tentercroft Av. Sys —5C **24**
Tetbury Dri. Shep —3B **8**
Thatchers Corner. E Gos
—2D **24**
Thirlemere Rd. Bar S —4H **13**
Thirlmere Dri. Lou —4C **10**
Thirlmere Rd. Bar S —5H **13**
Thistle Clo. Crop —6D **20**
Thomas St. Lou —2B **12**
Thompson Clo. Quor —1D **14**
Thornby Clo. Lou —5D **4**
Thorpe Acre Rd. Lou —1D **10**
Thorpe Hill. Lou —2C **10**
Thorpe Rd. Shep —2C **8**
Thresher's Wlk. E Gos —2D **24**
Thrussington Rd. Rat W
—5C **18**
Thrussington Rd. Thrus
—1H **19**
Thurcaston La. Roth —5F **21**
Tickow La. Shep —4A **8**
Tinkers Dell. E Gos —1D **24**
Tiverton Rd. Lou —6F **11**
Toller Rd. Quor —2C **14**
Toothill Rd. Lou —6H **5**
Towles Fields. Bur W —6G **7**
Town Grn. St. Roth —4A **22**
Town Hall Pass. Lou —2H **11**
Town Sq. Shopping Cen. Sys
—5B **24**
Trelissick Clo. Lou —6B **4**
Trinity Clo. Sys —6B **24**
Trinity St. Lou —2A **12**
True Lovers Wlk. Lou —1F **11**
Trueway Dri. Shep —3E **9**
Trueway Dri. S. Shep —3E **9**
Tuckers Clo. Lou —3A **12**
Tuckers Rd. Lou —3A **12**
Tuckett Rd. Wood E —4B **14**
Turner Av. Lou —3G **11**
Turner Clo. Quor —6D **12**
Turn St. Sys —5A **24**
Turvey La. Long W —1F **3**
Tyler Av. Lou —6F **5**
Tyler Ct. Shep —5E **3**
Tynedale Rd. Lou —5C **10**

Ullswater Av. Bar S —4H **13**
Ulverscroft Rd. Lou —5E **11**
Unitt Rd. Quor —3F **15**
University Clo. Sys —6B **24**
University Rd. Lou —3C **10**
Up. Church St. Sys —5B **24**
Upper Grn. Lou —5D **10**

Valley Rd. Lou —5E **11**
Val Wilson Ct. Lou —3B **10**

Vicarage Clo. Sys —5B **24**
Victoria Rd. Wood E —6B **14**
Victoria St. Lou —2H **11**
Victoria St. Quor —1E **15**
Victoria St. Sys —6B **24**
Village Rd. Nor S —1D **4**
Vinehouse Clo. Thurc —6F **21**
Vinetree Ter. Hot —2G **7**

Wain Dri. Lou —5C **4**
Walkers La. Roth —4A **22**
Walkers Way. Sys —5B **24**
Wallace Dri. Sile —6E **17**
Wallace Rd. Lou —3G **11**
Wallis Clo. Thurc —6F **21**
Walnut Rd. Lou —5G **11**
Walton La. Bar S —1F **13**
Walton Way. Mount —6H **15**
Wanlip Rd. Sys —6F **23**
Wards Cres. Sile —4E **17**
Wards End. Lou —2G **11**
Warner Pl. Lou —1A **12**
Warner's La. Lou —1H **11**
Warner St. Bar S —6H **13**
Warren, The. E Gos —2D **24**
Warwick Av. Quor —1C **14**
Warwick Way. Lou —6D **4**
Watchcrete Av. Quen —4D **24**
Watergate. E Gos —2E **25**
Water La. Sea —1A **18**
Waterside Clo. Lou —5H **5**
Watling Rd. Mount —5A **16**
Waugh's Dri. Mount —1H **21**
Wayfarer Dri. E Gos —1E **25**
Weaver Clo. Lou —4A **12**

Weaver's Wynd. E Gos —2D **24**
Welcome Stranger Caravan Pk.
    Sys —5B **24**
Weldon Av. Sile —3F **17**
Weldon Rd. Lou —5E **5**
Welland Rd. Bar S —1H **15**
Wellbrook Av. Sile —4F **17**
Wellington St. Lou —2A **12**
Wellington St. Sys —6A **24**
Wellsic La. Roth —3A **22**
Wellyard Clo. Shep —2E **9**
Wesley Clo. Hath —2A **4**
Wesley Clo. Lou —5B **4**
W. Cross La. Roth & Mount
    —2G **21**
Westfield Clo. Rear —1G **25**
Westfield Dri. Lou —2E **11**
Westfield La. Roth —4F **21**
Westmorland Av. Lou —4D **10**
Westoby Clo. Shep —1E **9**
W. Orchard. Sile —6E **17**
West St. Sys —6A **24**
Wetherby Clo. Quen —3E **25**
Whaddon Dri. Lou —4A **12**
Whall Clo. Quor —2E **15**
Wharncliffe Rd. Lou —2A **12**
Whatton Rd. Long W —1F **3**
Wheatland Dri. Lou —4A **12**
Whitby Clo. Lou —5B **4**
White Ga. Lou —6A **6**
Whitehouse Av. Lou —3A **12**
White St. Quor —1D **14**
Wicklow Clo. Shep —3E **9**
Wide La. Hath —2A **4**
Wide St. Hath —2A **4**
Widon, The. Lou —5E **11**

Wightman Clo. Shep —2D **8**
Wild Rose Wlk. E Gos —1E **25**
William Clo. Quen —3E **25**
William St. Lou —2G **11**
Willowcroft. Quor —2C **14**
Willow Gro. Mount —6G **15**
Willow Rd. Bar S —4H **13**
Willow Rd. Lou —5G **11**
Willows, The. Bur W —6G **7**
Willow Wlk. Sys —6H **23**
Wilmington Ct. Lou —3A **12**
Wilstone Clo. Lou —2C **10**
Wilton Av. Lou —4A **12**
Windermere Rd. Bar S —5H **13**
Windleden Rd. Lou —3B **10**
Windmill Clo. Mount —4A **16**
Windmill End. Roth —2A **22**
Windmill Rise. Wood E —5B **14**
Windmill Rd. Lou —2B **12**
Windsor Clo. Mount —1H **21**
Windsor Clo. Quor —1F **15**
Windsor Dri. Shep —3C **8**
Windsor Rd. Lou —6D **4**
Winterburn Way. Lou —2B **10**
Woburn Clo. Lou —1C **10**
Wolds, The. E Gos —2E **25**
Wollaton Av. Lou —1C **10**
Wolsey Way. Lou —1A **12**
Wolsey Way. Sys —6H **23**
Wood Clo. Shep —2F **9**
Woodfield Rd. Roth —3A **22**
Woodgate. Lou —2H **11**
Woodgate. Roth —3A **22**
Woodgate Dri. Lou —3F **11**
Woodhouse La. Nan —6A **10**

Woodhouse Rd. Quor —3A **14**
Woodlands Dri. Lou —4G **11**
Woodlands Dri. Shep —6E **3**
Wood La. Quor —2F **15**
Woodman's Chase. E Gos
    —2D **24**
Woodmans Way. Shep —6E **3**
Woodside. Bar S —5G **13**
Woodthorpe Av. Lou —4H **11**
Woodthorpe Rd. Lou —4H **11**
Woodward Av. Quor —1C **14**
Wordsworth Rd. Lou —1D **10**
Wortley Clo. Shep —6E **3**
Wortley Ct. Lou —1H **11**
Wreake Dri. Rear —4G **19**
Wren Clo. Sys —5G **23**
Wrights Clo. Quor —1D **14**
Wycliffe Av. Bar S —5H **13**
Wymeswold La. Bur W —5H **7**
Wymeswold Rd. Hot —1G **7**
Wyndale Dri. Sys —4B **24**
Wyndham Rd. Lou —5B **4**
Wythburn Clo. Lou —4D **10**
Wyvernhoe Dri. Quor —2C **14**

Yeoman's Dale. E Gos
    —1D **24**
York Clo. Mount —1H **21**
York Rd. Lou —1G **11**

Zouch Rd. Hath —1H **3**